COLORADO

NEBRASKA

IOWA

MISSOURI

KANSAS

Tipton

St. Louis

Springfield

OKLAHOMA

Fayetteville

Ft. Smith

TEXAS

Blackburn's

Boggy Depot

Waddell's

ARKANSAS

Nail's

Sherman

MISSISSIPPI

Earhart's

Gainesville

LOUISIANA

Delaware Springs

Pope's Camp

Skillman's

Emigrant Crossing

Llano Estacado

Ft Chadbourne

Clear Fork

Ft. Belknap

Relay

Head of Concho

Ft. Phantom Hill

Memphis

THE COLORFUL BUTTERFIELD OVERLAND STAGE

Reproductions

in Color of

21 Paintings

by

Marjorie Reed

From the Collection of

The James S. Copley Library

Text by

Richard F. Pourade

Introduction by

Richard B. Yale

A COPLEY BOOK

OTHER COPLEY BOOKS

ISBN: 0-913938-25-4

INTRODUCTION

James Marshall's 1848 gold discovery in California triggered a world-wide maelstrom, whose vortex drew gold-seekers, merchants, tradesmen, settlers and outlaws into all California.

By the mid-1850's their demands for a fast, safe and dependable means of overland transportation and communication with the eastern United States reached a crescendo that finally surmounted sectional differences in the Congress.

In 1857 a mail contract was awarded James Birch's "San Antonio and San Diego" line, which was described by one writer as the "line that started in the middle and didn't go anywhere." Jealous Angelenos termed it the "Jackass Mail."

The steamship routes via Panama, Nicaragua, Tehuantepec and Cape Horn were hazardous, or undependable, with some operators flourishing in their monopoly.

In March 1857 the Congress passed an act, sponsored jointly by Senator William McKendree Gwinn of California and Representative John Smith Phelps of Missouri, which authorized President James Buchanan and Postmaster General Aaron Venable Brown to contract for conveyance of the mail from such point on the Mississippi River as the contractors might select, to San Francisco, in the State of California.

Bids were advertised for, and in response nine competitive bids were received—three of these from John Butterfield and his associates. One of his bids provided for a semi-weekly service to operate from St. Louis and Memphis, converging at the most suitable point, to be located after a careful investigation, and then follow a designated route to San Francisco. This was called the "Bifurcated Route." Northern and Southern interests were both placated by the twin terminals. Further differences were probably conciliated by the intervention of Butterfield's friend, President Buchanan, and the great overland mail contract was signed and sealed on September 16, 1857.

In part the contract provided for: "...transporting the entire letter mail...from the Mississippi River to San Francisco, California, as follows: from St. Louis, Missouri, and Memphis, Tennessee, converging at Fort Smith, Arkansas, thence to El Paso, Tucson, Fort Yuma, Los Angeles and San Francisco, California, and back, twice a week in good four-horse post-coaches and spring wagons, suitable for the conveyance of passengers as well as the safety and security of the mails at $600,000 a year for the term of six years…" It also provided that service commence within twelve months after signing the contract.

Adoption of this route still brought protests from the North and East. However, most difficulties had been compromised or overcome. It proved to become the only route that could be safely driven over every day in the year from St. Louis to San Francisco.

The timing could not have been better for Butterfield's success. The new railroad and canal systems in the East had displaced the post roads and stage routes, thus making available a pool of experienced stage men for the new venture.

El Paso was established as the mid-point of two divisions and the route was divided into nine minor divisions, five east of El Paso and four to the west. A superintendent was appointed for each division and each superintendent was responsible for roads, stations, personnel, stock, forage and water supplies in his jurisdiction. The organization of the operating force consisted of conductors, drivers, station keepers, blacksmiths, mechanics, helpers and herders.

The route was approximately 2800 miles long, over which preliminary surveys were made, after which road crews were sent out both from East and West. Old roads were improved and new ones constructed. Favorable fording and ferrying places were located over streams and rivers. Over 1800 horses and mules were purchased and distributed over the route.

Three coach companies, Abbot and Downing, Concord, New Hampshire; James Goold Coach Company, Albany, New York; and Eaton, Gilbert and Company, Troy, New York built 250 coaches, freight and water wagons.

Two types of coaches were used: the famous "Concord" and the "Celerity" wagon, the latter an innovation of Butterfield to provide a lighter and faster type, not so subject to upset, for use on the rougher sections of the route.

On September 16, 1858, one year to the day, service was inaugurated in the East at Memphis and St. Louis and at San Francisco in the West. Butterfield took advantage of 160 miles of the new Pacific Railroad from St. Louis to Tipton, Missouri, where passengers and mail were transferred to the stage coaches.

The first west-bound mail arrived in San Francisco in twenty-three days, twenty-three hours and thirty minutes. The first east-bound run was made in twenty-four days, eighteen hours and twenty-six minutes.

Passenger fares west-bound were $200 and east-bound $100 but complaints of discrimination brought this to a uniform $200 both ways in 1859. Shortly thereafter the fare was reduced to $150 each way.

The route through California was both the roughest and most spectacular part of the journey. The San Joaquin Valley was either dusty beyond comprehension or a quagmire from swollen streams. Pacheco and Tejon Passes were too much for the six-horse teams and passengers invariably were compelled to walk up the grades, a custom that won a sobriquet of "Foot & Walker Line" for the service.

There was scarcely a bridge between San Francisco and Arkansas. In California most streams were forded; however the Kern, Kings and Colorado Rivers were ferried.

Employee discipline was rigid; conductors, drivers and station agents were generally noted for their courtesy, but once "on board" making time took priority over passenger comfort, and the conductor's call of "straighten yourselves up" meant "wake up and hang on, the going is getting rough."

The coaches ran 24 hours a day with probably two meal stops daily. The fare was rough and varied according to local supplies, consisting of game meats, beef, goat or mule meat, lots of beans, potatoes, coffee, tea and rarely milk and butter. A traveler, W. L. Ormsby, stated "it wasn't exactly like eating at the Waldorf." The stews were called "slumgullion" and the water was generally bad.

Recommended equipment for the transcontinental passenger was a pair of blankets, revolver or knife, an overcoat, some wine to mix with the water, and three or four dollars worth of provisions purchased at Los Angeles or Yuma to last over the desert.

One of the best contemporary accounts of stage travel via the Butterfield Overland Mail is contained in Ormsby's accounts of his trip on the first east to west run, published in *The New York Herald*. For a more detailed, scholarly account, Roscoe P. and Margaret B. Conkling's modern day three-volume work, "Butterfield Overland Mail," is most complete.

In the spring of 1861, secession and the Civil War forced suspension of the Overland Mail on the Southern Route. Personnel, stock and equipment were transferred to the Central Route. By 1869 the telegraph and railroad brought the era of transcontinental staging to a close.

In Postmaster General Brown's final report he praised the triumphant success of the Overland Mail. His report also included the detailed report of G. Bailey, the department's agent and a passenger on the first east-bound stage, who stated in part: "...it may be curious to those who, in later times, may be desirous to know by what energy, skill and perseverance the vast wilderness was penetrated by the mail stages of the United States, and the two great oceans united by the longest and most important land route ever established in any country."

Richard B. Yale
Editor and Publisher of the
Butterfield Express
and
Curator of the San Diego Union
Newspaper Museum

THE ARTIST

Marjorie Reed (now Marjorie Reed Creese) was inspired to paint by her father and was taught by Jack Wilkinson Smith, the noted landscape artist, who quickly became aware of her love for the outdoors, horses in action, and for western history. He encouraged her to roam the countryside, where she became acquainted with Capt. William Banning, who had been a stage driver for his father, the famed Phinneas Banning. From him she acquired a knowledge of stage coaches and the handling of teams of horses and, most importantly, of the Butterfield Overland Mail. Enthralled by the line's romantic history, and prepared after twenty years of study and research, she followed the Butterfield trail and began work on a series of paintings to record its story in form and color. Thus the paintings in this book show how it was to ride the Butterfield stage on the difficult run from San Francisco to the Yuma crossing on the Colorado River.

Most of these paintings are on exhibit at La Casa del Zorro in the Anza-Borrego Desert State Park.

THE PAINTINGS

LEAVING SAN FRANCISCO

East-bound Butterfield stages left San Francisco from Portsmouth Square, the historic Yerba Buena Plaza of Spanish days, where were located many of the ticket offices of California's pioneer stage lines.

The gentle contours of San Francisco's hills are etched in the haze of morning as the stage pulls away on its journey of twenty-one to twenty-four days. Day and night, over mountain passes, across desert sand, through Indian frontier land, past Army forts, from stagecoach stop to outpost village, the Butterfield rolled, covering an amazing average of 120 miles each day of the trip.

Passengers slept while they rode and the stages stopped at about 200 stations along the route only long enough for a change of drivers and horses or mules, and for two meals a day.

MISSION DOLORES

The route out of San Francisco led along the old Mission trail, or El Camino Real, rutted by the carettas of the Spanish era. The stage soon passed the little village then clustering around Mission San Francisco de Asis, popularly known as Mission Dolores, founded in 1776, the year of the Declaration of Independence by thirteen English speaking colonies on the east coast.

This scene was sketched in moonlight and touched up the following morning. The Mission still stands. From there the stage rolled down the peninsula along a line of ranches where homes served as road houses, and then headed down the rich Santa Clara Valley by way of San Jose and Gilroy and toward the first mountain pass.

MAKING TIME

Artist Marjorie Reed labeled this painting "Making Time." The horses are dashing over the crest of a hill against a brilliant sunset sky. Passengers invariably insisted that the "jehu"—affectionate term for the stage driver—was more interested in fast time on the road than in the comfort of the traveler and the welfare of the baggage.

The jehu lived and drove by John Butterfield's maxim: "Remember, boys, nothing on God's earth must stop the United States mail." The hill indicates that the country is getting rougher and that days soon would seem to grow longer and the nights more tiring.

OVER THE PACHECO PASS

A hundred miles out of San Francisco, near Gilroy, the stages reached a junction of the California coach road system. The main Butterfield route left the Mission road for the first real test of horse and passenger — the twelve-mile Pacheco Pass which leads eastward through the Diablo, or Devils Range, into California's central valleys.

The artist followed the almost obliterated coach tracks in the area of Pacheco Pass and could imagine the male passengers pushing and the women and children walking behind as the team, once more increased to six horses, strained to pull the heavy Concord coach. To Waterman Lily Ormsby II, who made the first westbound trip as a correspondent for the New York *Herald,* the road here led "over hills piled on hills."

TULE RIVER CROSSING

The main line run, however, which went down the San Joaquin Valley, the rich but baked plain which someday would be an agricultural empire, presented a panorama of vast and lonely stretches. Visalia, with 500 population, was the only town of any size. One welcome relief was the crossing of the shallow Tule River, a halfway point in the valley.

The artist once spent a summer on the Tule River hiking and exploring, and in later years old timers assisted her in re-creating the scene and the old stage buildings. Since the days of the Butterfield stage the river has changed its channel and the station site now is believed to be within the business district of the town of Porterville.

FOUNTAIN SPRINGS

On an average stations were about twenty miles apart, though the distances ranged from as little as nine to as much as sixty miles. Fourteen miles below the Tule River crossing was the Fountain Springs station where the artist said she found the old barn which had sheltered the horses and where the stages often met on their opposite journeys.

Here she painted her conception of the lively activity of "putting to the team." Soon after leaving Fountain Springs the stages entered a region of barren eroded hills and after crossing the rapidly running Kern River by flatboat and the swamps of the Tejon sink, approached the juncture of the Sierra Nevada and the coastal ranges which enclose the central valley.

WELCOME AT FORT TEJON

In the fact and fiction of the West, mountain passes provided the most favorable situation for holdups.

After ascending spiraling Grapevine Canyon in the Tehachapi Mountains, the stage reached the summit of the often cold and windy Tejon Pass and received the welcome of Fort Tejon.

The fort was established in 1854 primarily to control the Indians, as well as to protect the pass against any marauders.

In their study of the Butterfield route, Roscoe P. and Margaret B. Conkling described it as surrounded by timbered and verdue-covered mountains, with springs of sweet water nearby — one of the most beautiful of all Army posts.

Before it became a stage stop it was made an experimental station for the Army's Camel Corps with which the government had hoped to conquer the desert.

HOLDUP IN FREMONT PASS

Mauraders gave Fort Tejon a wide berth and sought out other less-guarded passes at which they could ambush the unwary traveler. The route after leaving Fort Tejon followed a different course than the highway of today.

Avoiding the present Ridge Route by swinging easterly at Gorman and crossing over onto the dry side of the mountains, the stage followed the high western rim of the Mojave Desert through Antelope Valley to Lake Elizabeth. From there it turned south through San Francisquito Canyon to Saugus and finally began the descent toward the Los Angeles basin, by way of the short but stiff San Fernando, or Fremont Pass. In this scene holdup men wait below the sharp cut which had been made in the mountain ridge to facilitate early-day transportation of military vehicles and wheeled cannon.

HOLDUP FOR RINCON PAYROLL

The Butterfield company had strict rules against passengers carrying large sums of money, and the more serious holdups took place on the alternate coastal route, where one traveler reported the finding of seven bodies.

The coastal line, however, maintained excellent mail and passenger service between Los Angeles and San Francisco and Butterfield also had a close working relationship with Wells, Fargo throughout all of California.

Wells, Fargo express boxes and mining and ranch payrolls were tempting targets, to be seized at some convenient coastal point of surprise in Cuesta Pass, on a sudden turn on rugged Rincon Point, or along the remote roads connecting the interior mines of Southern California as well as those of Northern California with the main stage lines, and which so often were frequented by roving bands of killers.

MISSION SAN FERNANDO

Back on the main route and upon emerging from San Fernando Pass into San Fernando Valley, the Butterfield stage passengers came to a new aspect of country and vegetation and a population which retained more of the Spanish and Mexican element than did Northern California.

Correspondent Ormsby wrote that part of the old San Fernando Mission was being used as a stable for the company's horses and he saw a few giggling Indian women washing their clothes as "we passed with our beautiful team of six white horses." The stage was back once more on El Camino Real, trod by Father Junipero Serra in founding the chain of California missions.

LOS ANGELES

It was up and over the short Cahuenga Pass, and then, in the words of an English traveler, William Tallack, "The sunny plains and vineyards of Ciudad de los Angeles were now spread before us, whilst in the foreground rose, in the light of the sunset, the purple sierras of San Gorgonio."

The conductor's bugle heralded their approach to Los Angeles at the end of the first division on the eastward run, eighty hours and 460 miles from San Francisco. Los Angeles then was a town of 5000. For those who wanted to linger there were, for a time, accommodations at the Bella Union Hotel. The Church of Our Lady of the Angels is the centerpiece for the largest of the paintings of this series (five by six feet), and a composition of much action under a hazy Southern California sky.

THE BROKEN WHEEL

After leaving Los Angeles the Butterfield stages once more swung away from El Camino Real and soon were pounding down the southern immigrant trail over which had passed thousands of persons in the Gold Rush of 1849. For a hundred miles, by way of today's El Monte, Lake Elsinore and Temecula, it followed a series of interior valleys slowly rising toward the normal snow line but always keeping just below it.

Roads did not have to be steep to be rough. One correspondent described how a nigh wheel horse stumbled and was dragged twenty feet. Shortly after a crossbar broke. It had been made of pine instead of oak. Coaches intended for mountain travel were made stronger but, as this painting depicts, broken wheels were common.

WARNER'S PASS

By the late 1850's there was little fight left in the Indians of Southern California, if there ever had been much. Here a family watches pensively as the Butterfield stage lurches through a narrow valley on the approach to Puerta de la Cruz, or the Port of the Cross. They were up 3000 feet now and running just below San Diego's high mountain peaks, in a country of gnarled oaks and huge boulders.

The Port of the Cross is the entrance of the Valley of San Jose, which lies at the upper end of the mountain gateway into Southern California from the Colorado Desert. Just above the site of this painting is the Oak Grove station, which has been preserved, and while there have been enlargements and alterations, it still retains the atmosphere of the old staging days. It is located on the roadside of California State Highway 79, in eastern San Diego County.

WARNER'S RANCH

In San Jose Valley the Overland Mail by-passed the nearby hot springs and headed directly for the lights of Warner's, once the most welcome and most famous of the stopping places on the old southern immigrant trail. Here always were to be found food, warmth and supplies.

It originally was built by J. J. Warner, an American who had become a Mexican citizen, as a trading post on his huge Mexican land grant, at the point where the road to San Diego forked off from the main immigrant route to Los Angeles and San Francisco. Later abandoned, it was rehabilitated and converted into a Butterfield station and still stands as a memorial on one of America's most historic trails.

Marjorie Reed

SAN FELIPE VALLEY

Soon after leaving Warner's, the Butterfield stages crossed a ridge of the watershed, where on one side the waters drained toward the Pacific Ocean and on the other toward the Gulf of California.

From there the road turned down the east side of the coastal mountain range by way of San Felipe Valley, the green upper desert side of the southern gateway to California. This was the trail followed by General Stephen Watts Kearny's weary Army of the West during the Conquest of California in 1846. The vaqueros driving half-wild cattle, the Indians in their melon patches and snow-clad Volcan Mountain in the background presented a pastoral scene soon to be left behind.

BOX CANYON

At the bottom of the San Felipe Valley the Butterfield stages came to the end of green country and to the edge of the high desert and raced along hard flat land slanting downward through dry Earthquake Valley.

At its end they came to one of the wonders of the 2800-mile route, Box Canyon. This was a narrow chasm two and a half miles long which, over the ages, flash floods had cut through a rocky ledge guarding the entrance to the next desert, Mason Valley. In 1847 the Mormon Battalion, while opening a wagon road to California during the Mexican War, had to hack away at the rocky sides to enable their wagons to squeeze through. To one correspondent the roadway was a marvel of nature. Another wrote that if God ever represented this part of the earth as good it was more than man had ever done.

VALLECITO

On the edge of the lower desert was Vallecito, the little valley, an oasis that to westbound passengers meant that the long lonely ride across the wastes of Arizona and the Colorado Desert was at last behind them. It was a "beautiful green spot" of about five miles square with a number of springs, some of them salty, and surrounded by rugged timberless hills.

The caretaker of the restored stage station at Vallecito put lighted kerosene lamps in the windows to inspire the artist to a more realistic interpretation of the desolate yet fascinating scene. Here, the east-bound "coach and six" pulls away from the artistic adobe as the station keeper waves farewell. No one ever forgot Vallecito. It was the beginning as well as the end of the desert.

AGUA CALIENTE

The Carrizo Corridor is a great natural desert pathway. From Vallecito, east-bound stages ran down the gently sloping corridor, which had occasional but vital watering holes, and then dropped into the Imperial Valley, in those days a forbidding, uncultivated land below the level of the sea.

For west-bound stages, the corridor was the way out of the desert after the dry run from Yuma. At its western end the corridor connected with the only low-level route through the coastal mountain barrier.

In this painting the artist depicts a meeting of east and west stages in the sandy wash of Agua Caliente in the corridor between Vallecito and the Carrizo Creek stations. But the schedule permitted no delays for exchange of gossip and each driver hoped to break the record of twenty-one days between Tipton, the railroad end west of St. Louis, and San Francisco.

THE WATER OF LIFE

Long before the name of Palm Springs had become attached to a famed resort in the desert, Palm Springs was merely a spot in the desert on the Butterfield run, on the eastern edge of what is now San Diego County, far south of the town that someday would bear the same name.

Unbearably hot in summer, it nevertheless represented the water of life to weary passengers and horses.

Ormsby, going west, wrote that at Palm Springs, "...we met the fifth stage from San Francisco, which was a little behind the usual time, but ahead of schedule today."

In 1853 the scientist W. P. Blake described the little desert springs and the three or four palm trees, each standing about thirty feet high. Others had been destroyed by passing immigrant trains.

Thirty years ago only a solitary stump remained. Today, there are two fine trees and the spring is running.

CARRIZO INDIAN RAID

The stations now were stark outposts, where desert Indians gave keepers a great deal of trouble by running off stock and occasionally getting up enough courage for open attacks which seldom succeeded.

Here is the Carrizo Creek station, in a country yet untamed by civilization. The correspondent Ormsby told of an emigrant train which had just passed and the Butterfield passengers met numbers of cattle which had been abandoned as being too weak to travel, and ". . . there they stood, almost living skeletons, gradually dying of thirst, with water within a few miles of them." Often a half or two thirds of the westward-bound cattle droves were left on the road, to gasp away their lives or perhaps to be butchered by roving Indians.

ON TO YUMA CROSSING

After leaving Carrizo station the stage experienced heavy going across the desert floor to Indian Wells, occasionally, too, encountering parties of United States soldiers covered with dust, on patrol along the edges of Yuma and Apache Indian country. The road soon dipped into Mexico to avoid the sand hills west of the Colorado River, and the horses were watered at Alamo Mocho and Cooke's Wells.

The ride quickened with the approach to the Colorado over higher and harder ground covered with mesquite. Soon the stages pulled up at Jaeger's ferry crossing on the California side, downstream from Fort Yuma. Across the river was the collection of adobe houses known as Arizona City, now Yuma. This was the end of the second division, 740 miles or so and 150 hours from San Francisco.

Beyond the river lay the Gila Trail across Arizona, and over the far distant horizon were the beckoning lights of St. Louis, and beyond them the attractions of the sophisticated states that bordered the Atlantic. The Far West no longer was a land of tomorrow.

Some of the stage stops along the Butterfield, 1858.

CALIFORNIA

NEVADA

UTAH

ARIZONA

NEW MEXICO

San Francisco
San Mateo
Clark's Redwood City
Seventeen Mile House
San Jose Gilroy
Pacheco Pass San Luis Ranch
Lone Willow Firebaugh's Ferry
Fresno City Elkhorn
Whitmore's Ferry Visalia
Packwood Tule River
Fountain Spring Mountain House
Poso Creek Gordon's Ferry
River Slough Sink of Tejon
Kern Reed's Ft. Tejon
Widow Smith's French John's
Mission San Fernando Hart's
Los Angeles Cahuenga
Rancho San Jose El Monte
Temescal Chino Ranch
Laguna Grande Temecula
Oak Grove Aguanga
San Felipe Warner's Ranch
Palm Springs Vallecito
Hall's Well Carrizo
Alamo Mocho Indian Wells
Yuma Cooke's Wells
Mohawk Filibuster Camp
Murderer's Grave Flapjack Ranch
Picacho Pass Gila Ranch
Tucson Cienega
Stein's Peak
Apache Pass Lordsburg
Mesilla
Las Cruces Cottonwoods
Ft. Fillmore Hueco Tanks
El Paso

Pacific Ocean